Learning About Life Cycles

The Life Cycle of a

Rose

Ruth Thomson

PowerKiDS
press

New York

Published in 2009 by The Rosen Publishing Group Inc.
29 East 21st Street, New York, NY 10010

Copyright © 2009 Wayland/The Rosen Publishing Group, Inc.

First Edition

Editor: Victoria Brooker
Designer: Simon Morse
Consultant: Michael Scott OBE, B.Sc

Library of Congress Cataloging-in-Publication Data

Thomson, Ruth, 1949-
  The life cycle of a rose / Ruth Thomson. — 1st ed.
      p. cm. — (Learning about life cycles)
  Includes index.
  ISBN 978-1-4358-2837-7 (library binding) —
  ISBN 978-1-4358-2887-2 (paperback)
  ISBN 978-1-4358-2893-3 (6-pack)
  1. Roses—Life cycles—Juvenile literature. I. Title. II. Series:
  Thomson, Ruth, 1949- Learning about life cycles (PowerKids
  Press)
  QK495.R78T46 2009
  635.9'33734—dc22

                                    2008025768

Manufactured in China

Photographs: Cover (inset mr and br), 3, 7, 8, 12, 14,
18, 20, 21, 23tl, 23 br, 23bl naturepl.com; Cover
(main) Mark Hicken/Alamy; Cover (inset tr),
10 Brian Hoffman/Alamy; 2 Imagebroker/Alamy;
4-5 Stone Nature Photography/Alamy; 6 Frank
Blackburn/Alamy; 9 Michael Wheatley/Alamy;
11, 23tr Marilyn Shenton/Alamy; 13 Leonid
Serebrennikov/Alamy; 15 Premaphotos/Alamy;
16, 19 WoodyStock/Alamy; 17 Organica/Alamy;
22 blickwinkel/Alamy.

Web Sites

Due to the changing nature of
Internet links, PowerKids Press has
developed an online list of Web sites
related to the subject of this book.
This site is updated regularly.
Please use this link to access this list
www.powerkidslinks.com/lalc/rose

Contents

Roses grow here

People plant roses in yards, gardens, and parks. Wild roses grow in hedges in the countryside.

What is a rose?

A rose is a flowering plant. They usually have stems with sharp **thorns**. Garden roses have large, colorful flowers. Many have a strong, sweet smell.

A garden rose ▶

leaf

petal

stem

A wild rose ▲

thorn

Wild roses have
smaller flowers.
This book looks
at wild roses.

7

Seeds and shoots

Rose plants grow from **seeds**. In the spring, warm weather and rain help the seed to sprout. Slowly, a shoot pushes up through the ground.

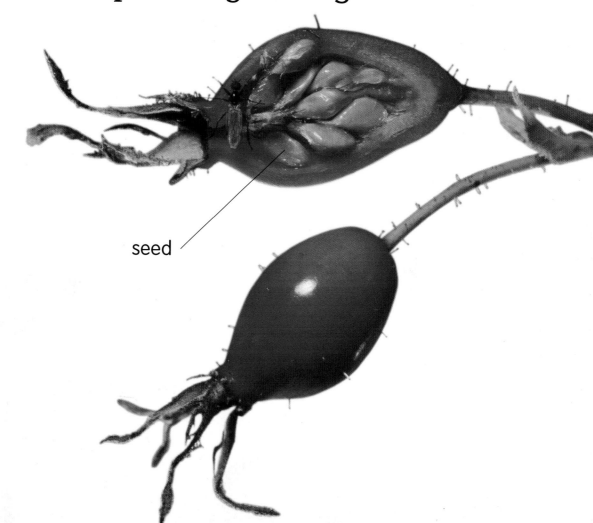

seed

The new plant grows bigger and bigger. It climbs up a hedge or tree to reach the light. Its **thorns** help it to hang on.

May

Buds

New leaves appear. New flower **buds** begin to grow.

Green **sepals** protect the flower buds.
Soon the sepals open out, showing
the petals inside.

sepal

Flowers

Each flower has five petals with a sweet scent. It also has a sweet liquid called **nectar**.

June-August

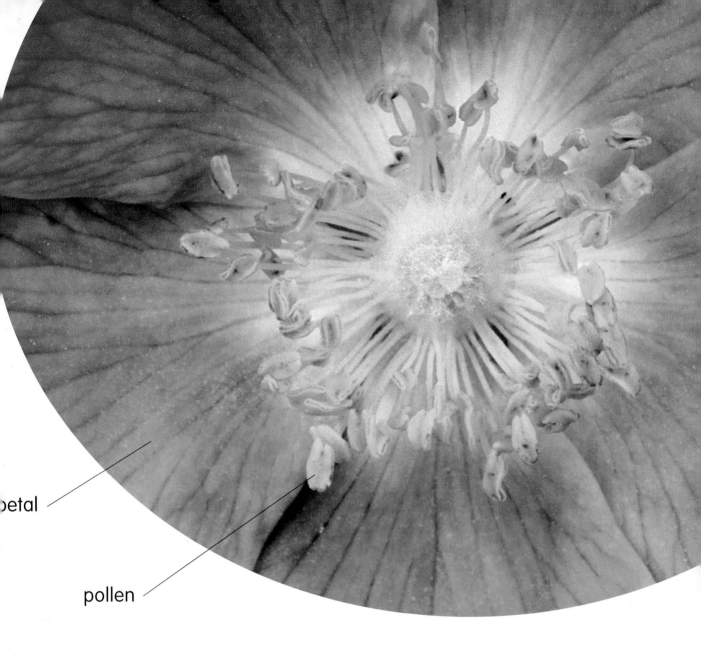

petal

pollen

The flowers produce tiny grains
called **pollen**. This is needed to
make **seeds**.

Pollination

A flower's scent attracts insects, such as beetles, flies, and bees. As they feed on the **nectar**, **pollen** sticks to them.

When an insect goes to another flower, pollen from the first flower rubs off onto the next one. This is called pollination.

Receptacle

After pollination, the flower no longer needs to attract insects. Its petals fall off.

The top part of the stem, called the receptacle, starts to swell. **Seeds** begin to grow inside it.

receptacle

Rosehip

The receptacle swells more and turns red. When it is ripe, it is called a rosehip.

he rosehip is packed with **seeds**.
hese have a very tough coat
o protect them.

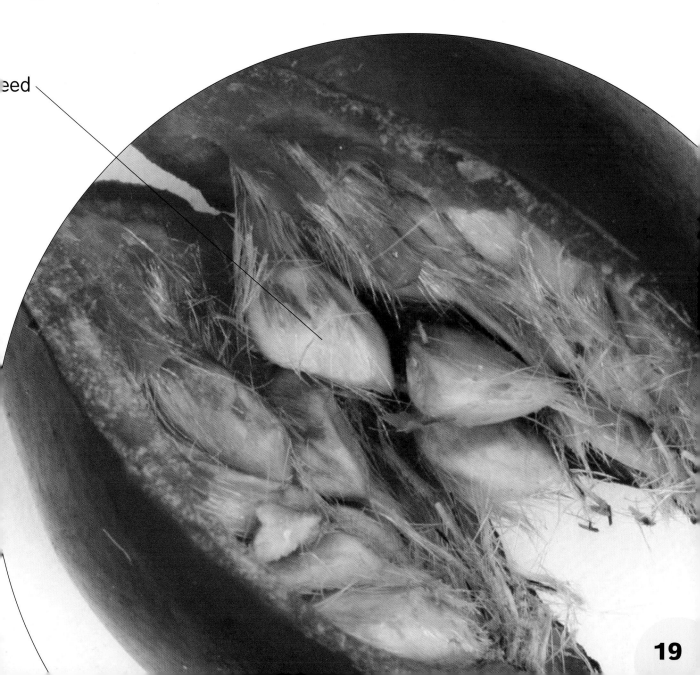

eed

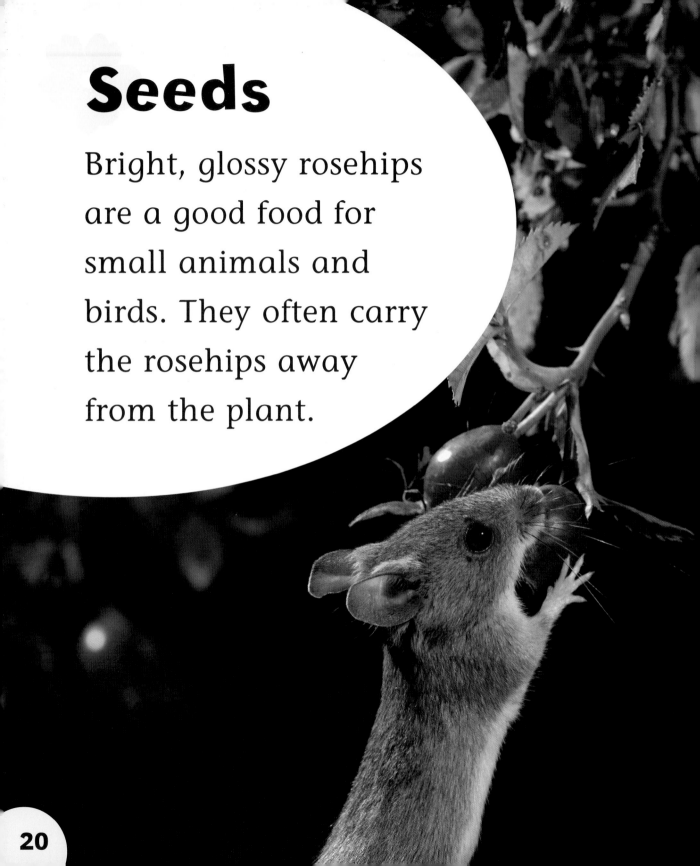

Seeds

Bright, glossy rosehips are a good food for small animals and birds. They often carry the rosehips away from the plant.

The **seeds** come out unharmed
in bird and animal droppings.
They may land on soil where they
can grow into new rose plants.

Fall and winter

The rosehips stay on the plant at the beginning of winter. They make a tasty meal for hungry birds and are soon eaten up. In the spring, new leaves begin growing again.

Rose life cycle

Seed
In the spring, a tiny
seed starts to grow
into a new plant.

Buds
Leaf and flower
buds appear on
the plant.

Rosehip
After a flower is pollinated,
a rosehip starts to form.
Seeds are growing inside.

Flowers
The flower
buds open.

Glossary and Further Information

bud the part of a plant from which leaves or flowers develop

nectar   the sweet liquid inside many flowers that attracts insects

pollen the grains of powder in flowers needed to make new seeds

seed   the part of a plant that grows into a new plant

sepal the part of a plant that wraps around a bud to keep it safe before it opens

thorn   the hard, pointed part of a plant that grows on the stem

Books

The Life Cycle of a Flower
by Molly Aloian and Bobbie Kalman (Crabtree Publishing, 2004)

What is a Life Cycle?
by Bobbie Kalman (Crabtree Publishing, 1998)

Index